Lifestyle Reality Observing

It's A New Kind Of Life Coaching

I0427392

One of the problems facing the Life Coaching Industry is that it has a history of being confused by the public as a kind of Personal Counseling. This has led to chaos in the industry as Life Coach Training Programs try to distinguish themselves from Counselor Training Programs. There are serious ethical, civil and even criminal liabilities for people who practice Life Coaching and stray into the field of Personal Counseling. The issue is so rampant that some states are actually considering licensure or certification and or supervision of Life Coaches.

What follows is a discussion of a proposed new kind of Life Coaching. It is NOT a substitute for competent legal advice. It is NOT to be used as substitute for competent Life Coaching training. You make NOT use any of these ideas and turn around and sue me if it doesn't work out. This is just a discussion that will hopefully illuminate some of the critical issues facing our chosen career field.

I call my Life Coaching business and process, Lifestyle Reality Observing (LRO). Lifestyle Reality Observing is a set of powerful tools for coaching individuals and organization. LRO uses good observation, and communication skills; in order to help an individual or organization get where it wants to be.

Part of the reason there is such confusion about the difference between Life Coaching and Personal Counseling is that they look the same in many aspects. In fact many counselors see little or no difference. The problem is that there is a huge difference.

Personal Counseling deals with emotionally distressed clients. Mental Health Counseling deals with actual pathology which clients suffer. Life Coaching should only deal with high functioning clients who want to maximize the performance in a broad area of their lives.

While it is easy to see that counseling is serious stuff; few people appreciate that coaching is of great importance too. Each service serves the needs of clients.

I was a Registered Counselor for two decades and a Mental Health Counseling Associate for a year. I can assure you that all Life Coaching clients need competent services. I will spend the rest of this booklet describing the appropriate Life Coaching Client and various approaches one might use in Lifestyle Reality Observing to assist. The following examples are fictionalized examples of oh so real people.

All identifying characteristics have been carefully sanitized from the scenarios and if you think you know the person it is purely coincidental. This is done to protect their privacy and mine.

Lifestyle Reality Observing or LRO uses many of the high quality methods of communication which counselors use, but that is all, the two career fields have in common. In LRO we never prescribe a solution for the client. Not even if we see the answer so clearly. In LRO we believe that with sound feedback a client will own the answers at which they arrive. It is with the struggle to find the answers to their life's questions; that they gain the personal power to implement the changes they want. If we do the work for them; we cheat them out of the power and freedom they seek.

The Story of the Bored House Wife

Martha was bored. Her children were in college and she faced everyday at home with nothing to do but chores. She had what I call the "curse of the active intellect." Her husband was a sweat heart but he was absorbed in his work and usually exhausted when he was home.

Martha began to stay up most of the night playing on facebook. She went to her doctor but was denied sleeping pills because her doctor said there was nothing wrong with her except she needed to make some lifestyle changes and adjustments. Specifically he was concerned that she had gained 30 pounds since the last girl had moved out and gone to college

That's how I met Martha. At our first meeting she talked about wanting to do anything but stay home and do chores. She said that staying home all day and eating; or staying out all day and shopping were not satisfying.

I asked her to make a list of 10 things she has always wanted to do. She was to spare no expense and not care about the practicality of doing it. Her list was at first rather banal and uninteresting. I encouraged her to spend some time really brainstorming and get back to me when she had finished the assignment. She did finish the assignment and was quite eager to share it with me the following week. Her list was quite was now impressive and elaborate. She had numerous exotic places to visit and numerous rare experiences to be had. At the top of her list she wanted to visit Vanatu (a South Pacific island nation) and she wanted to fly on the Zero G airplane. The plane ride is where you get to experience zero gravity intermittently for about 30 minutes. I didn't know much about these two things so I suggested she do some research on the internet and figure out how she was going to get there. We did several telephone sessions and she decided she was also going to exercise and lose weight for the tropical beaches on Vanatu. She also decided to write an E-book about the whole adventure.

Eventually she located a Christian medical group that would take her to Vanatu if she was a certified nursing assistant and volunteered to work there.

So she went out and took the class and the internship at the local community college. She did go to Vanatu and did write a wonderful book and the modest royalties from the book paid for most of her Zero G flight about 3 years later. I think it cost $4,000.

The royalties now go to support the Vanatu medical group. I ran into Martha the other day. She was tan and lean and she mentioned she is still working on her list. She is never bored.

We find in LRO that once a person is unleashed by their self - imposed limitation; they are unstoppable. If I had said, "look Martha let's start off with something sensible like a trip to Florida"; I might have ruined it for her. It is not my job to share my opinion about her dreams. I have to admit Vanatu was out of my experience, and comfort; but that didn't make a difference. She is the one who became a medical missionary and got to go there!

The only time I was directive in our entire LRO relationship was in that I encouraged her to really let loose in her brainstorming and to investigate things on the internet. I never said Vanatu, where the heck is Vanatu? She never suffered from boredom again, and had a great LRO success story.

Ethics- A Code of Conduct for LRO Practitioners

I would like to suggest a Code of Conduct. It's not all inclusive but it does cover some of the basic ways one can mess up badly in LRO.

1. Dual Relationships. Don't have them.

2. Money should be cash up front.

3. Sharing personal problems. Don't.

4. Mental Health Issues. They should see someone else for mental health services.

5. Giving advice. Never

6. Confidentiality

7. Share the code with the client

Dual Relationships

The idea is to protect the client from an imbalance of power in the LRO relationship. They pay money to be empowered not to be slept with. It is your responsibility not to socialize with them.

Money

Getting paid upfront makes everything nice. Then there will be no checks that bounce or credit cards that get overdrawn or cancelled. It also motivates the client to use the time well. They are spending real money.

Personal Problems

Part of being a responsible RLO practitioner is to not share your personal problems with the clients. While you must be friendly you should not start a friendship. LRO clients tend to be likeable outgoing even exciting people but you have fiduciary relationship and it should stay that way. How long should you wait after the leave your services before you can have a friendship? I am just speculating but it seems at least five to seven years.

Mental Health Issues

Sometimes an LRO client may also have a mental health counselor. If your boundaries are clear and the mental health counselor approves and you can stay completely out of mental health issues; go for it. Counseling clients can benefit from LRO as long as the counselor feels comfortable with it.

Advice

Never give advice. The client will not grow into their solutions to their life questions and they may blame you when their choices lead to unforeseen consequences.

As LRO practitioners we don't give advice. We just act as a mirror for them to gain their own perspective. We listen and seemingly ask endless open ended questions. We have no hidden agenda.

Confidentiality

Keep their information, secrets, and opinions secret forever. Unless a client discloses a felony like child abuse; keep all their indiscretions a secret. I destroy any client notes after 7 years. All of us grow and change.

Share the Code of Conduct with the Client.

Make sure the client knows your Code of Conduct before you start. It makes it easier to resolve misunderstandings later.

So what goes on in a LRO session?

A Lifestyle Reality Observer carefully listens to the coaching client and then thoughtfully reflects the information back. Assumptions which the client has, are challenged only by asking for clarification. The client is challenged to get a clearer view of their life issues and possible solutions.

Here is an example. The first time I went to a life coach I was complaining about the amount of stress I was experiencing as a counselor. She asked one question that struck home and showed me the power of life coaching.

She asked, "do you have to experience stress to be a good counselor?" I said no. and then I understood the process we were using. I instantly lost that need to be stressed out because I care. Eventually I came to the conclusion that I owed it to my counseling clients to be the healthiest happy person I could be, in order to do a good job!

But the turning point in my lifestyle issue was that simple question. If I had said, " yes." She would have ask me how does being stressed out help me? I went to her to find a new career and end up doing 6 more years as a counselor because after that one session I was having so much fun.

That is how it is in LRO sessions. It is hard to make a living off of one client because if you are doing it right they will become empowered to make those lifestyle choices without you.

When I am acting as a counselor, I do a powerful form of counseling called Reality Therapy Control Theory. It was created by Dr. William Glasser. I can only think of 2 clients in 2 decades that needed my counseling more than 8 or 9 visits. But LRO is even tends to be even briefer. After 3 or 4 visits they are ready to be independent.

My door is always open for them to return but I have never had a LRO client return. They seem too busy living! You will have to make an income by the number happy word of mouth clients, not the duration of service given to individuals

How Much Should I Charge?

How much is a happy life worth? Your services are priceless but the market will only bear so much. Perhaps you can charge $50 to $150 an hour for in person one on one LRO. Maybe you can charge $50 to $75 an hour via phone or Skype. It is up to you and the client. I never work for less than $35 an hour. In general $50 dollars is the going rate, for a beginning LRO practitioner.

Groups depending on size, should be charged $500 to $1000 for a 4 hour day. This booklet will not address group work and how to get it.

Tom

Tom seemed like a natural LRO client. He was 28 years old. He had an extensive background in sales and had started up several in home online businesses. His home and love life were in disarray. His finances where in a shambles and he just couldn't seem to make much money; although his start- up businesses seemed to promise money. He was a part- time used car salesman. This job kept him at least out of the rain and in a triple wide mobile home. He proudly mentioned that he lived in the biggest mobile home in the park!

Tom wanted to make a real living. He was looking at a multi-level marketing company for the answer to his problems. He came to me to figure out if his career was headed in the right direction. He did not want to invest in one more fruitless endeavor.

Tom a hyper- active and intelligent man made our meetings exhausting for me. I just kept up with him by asking open ended questions, at least 50 an hour! I could not get him to reflect very deeply for very long.

In our third meeting I asked him only two questions. The first question was, "What thing does he really like to do the most?" For the first half hour he rambled and I repeatedly redirected him back to the question phrasing it a little differently. Slowly he came to the conclusion that he really enjoyed selling cars. He told me tales of making the sales and meeting interesting people. After a half hour dwelling on selling cars he decided that he would stop the other businesses and go full time into selling cars. He decided that working at home and alone was not the best thing for an energetic personality like him.

My next question was," Is his hyperactivity helpful or hurtful to his making a living." He became quite agitated with me. I explained that I was just asking the question. He would have to come up with the answer. So he spent 27 minutes telling how great it was to be hyperactive. The last three minutes he admitted that hyperactivity caused him to lose focus on his work and made it impossible for him to follow through on things. He said he did not want to take drugs to solve his problem.

I told him he would have to consult with a doctor or counselor about the whole issue of hyperactivity because I was just a LRO practitioner. It was out of my specialty and competence.

I could not get him to come in for another meeting for two months. Then one day he wanted a phone session at half cost. I accepted his offer and he was a changed man on the phone. I asked him what he had been up to.

He said that after our last meeting he went and got a second part- time job in car sales. It didn't go so well and within 2 weeks he was fired for being annoying to customers and other sales people.

In desperation he talked with his doctor and tried a low dose of a drug. It was perfect for him and he could think clearly for the first time in his life! He went back to the used car dealership which had fired him and got his job back!

He wanted to thank me for my help with LRO. I told him he did all the work.

Two years later he is a top sales person and lives in a house on the beach, with his wife. He is planning on starting his own car dealership. LRO clients are unstoppable.

Behind the scene

Tom was a difficult client to serve especially because I found used car salesman personality obnoxious. When he seized control of the process of LRO meetings, I almost gave him his money back and sessions one and two! My heart sank in session number three because I did not think I could stay true to the principle of LRO.

I became convinced that I just needed to refer him to a doctor or counselor during the last 27 minutes of session number three.

When it was my turn to talk I just said, he would have to seek help for his other needs elsewhere. I believe that because I used this approach; Tom did find his way. As all LRO clients find their way. When a LRO client can't find his or her own way; they were never an appropriate LRO client.

Mary

Mary was social butterfly. Her work and evening schedules were full continuously. Even on Sunday she went to church early and stayed late. The whole time she gossiped. She loved to know what was happening and she relish the private activities other people.

She hurt many people by what she said and what she didn't say. To some people she was a monster. Things came to a head when none of her dear friends would speak to her any more. Even her Christian friends who were duty bound to forgive said that they forgave her but would not provide her with a victim anymore.

The head of the local domestic violence agency actually described her as an abuser of other peoples trust. She was also described as emotional terrorist. Needless to say she was insulted and flabbergasted. After all she had gossiped for almost 40 years why should she change now?

Counselors in town wisely would not see her because she was a notorious liar. There was nobody in her very small community to help her.

I was reluctant to see her too but she paid $90 an hour and she wanted life coaching. Even after telling her about LRO; she wanted it. So we sat down and talked.

I told her that LRO was not therapy and it would not be helpful if she needed counseling. She was well funded and asked that I give it a try. So I did.

I restricted our conversation to one question and I repeated the question many times in our first meeting. I asked, "What do you really want? She told me numerous things but she just couldn't get past the superficial. Finally in the last two minutes of our meeting I asked," what does she really what in a friend."

I told her to make a list of 20 things that she wanted in a friend. I also told her that we couldn't meet until she had 20 real characteristics that she required in a friendship. She left somewhat confused but did the assignment for the next week.

The next week she rambled off the list and I made her clarify every trait she wanted in a friend. Through a process of open ended questioning she concluded that she must become the person who has all these traits, or she would never have a friend like this.

I told her I was willing to help her as an LRO practitioner but she must do the work.

We met once a month for six more months. The LRO meetings were intense and there were many tears because we explored all the hurtful things she had done and how she was becoming a new person.

She wanted to be person that didn't take advantage of information she had about people. She wanted to use information for the benefit of others. She decided she was going into politics! I suspended my judgment in session but had serious doubts about her success!

Although she lost several local elections; she eventually won a county political position by a landslide, two years later! She was almost universally loved even by her opponents by then. Her strategy which brought her to such success; was to admit when her behavior and thoughts were wrong. This is very rare in politics. I heard over the radio when she won her election. I cried.

Conclusion

LRO is powerful set of tools. It frees up the client to maximize their potential. I have continually astonished at how powerful a free person is to create their own way in the world.

Questions and Answers

Q. Where can I get Certified in LRO?

A. At this time the LRO Commons is not certifying practitioners. Look for information and a web presence in December 2014

Q. Who is the LRO Commons?

A. The LRO Commons is a group of like- minded mostly retired former mental health counselors who promote the principles of LRO.

Q. What will training in LRO cost?

A. The cost of Basic Level training will be very minimal as it will be online.

Q. Why would I take Basic LRO Training?

A. Basic LRO Training may give you a sound view of how life coaching is very different from counseling and how to avoid mixing the two techniques.

Q. Why can't I just read a book?

A. You can but practical applications are more likely to help you be successful.

Other Books by James Nugent

How I Sailed From Olympia to The San Juan Islands, and Returned Safely

An Alternative Boating Guide to Southern Puget Sound

How and Why I lived Aboard

Micro Refuges of Budd Inlet in South Puget Sound

I Speak Esperanto

The Rainbow Road and Other Signs of God's Love

Living an Abundant Life, Within Your Means

Social Jujitsu and Powerful Principles for Managing Social Conflict

Blackjack on My Small Budget

A Little Benedictine Oblate Manuel

Without Speech

All things work

Loving Time with Your Creator

Personal Adventures in a Life of Learning

The Good News about Being Catholic

E-book Writing and Overcoming Barriers to Creativity

E-book Writing and Organizing Your Ideas

My Forty Days For Life 2013

Winter Sailing in Southern Puget Sound

Available at Amazon.com in Kindle E-Book and or Audible Book or Paperback

Notes and Reflections

www.ingramcontent.com/pod-product-compliance
Lightning Source LLC
Chambersburg PA
CBHW072254310526
45795CB00011B/1133